IGNATIUS CRITICAL EDITIONS

Study Guide for
Macbeth

— *by William Shakespeare* —

Edited by
Eleanor Donlon
Joseph Pearce

Introduction by
Patrick S. J. Carmack

IGNATIUS PRESS　　　　　SAN FRANCISCO

Cover design by John Herreid

ISBN 978-1-58617-398-2

Printed in the United States of America ∞

Table of Contents

Why a Great Books Study Guide?

Wisdom is generally acknowledged to be the highest good of the human mind, whether this be recognized as knowledge of first principles and causes or as a contemplative gaze at Wisdom itself. But how does one obtain wisdom? The means is primarily conversation with great and wise persons who have already advanced far along the paths of knowledge and understanding to wisdom. As the philosopher Dr. Peter Redpath succinctly puts it when addressing audiences of young people interested in understanding why they ought to read great books, "If you wish to become wise, learn from wise people."

Since, however, persons of great wisdom are rare and generally unavailable to us due to distance or death, we enter into conversation with them through their books which record their thought. In doing this, we soon discover how all the authors of great books used this same method of study themselves. They began by conversing with or reading the great books written by the sages of earlier generations. In so doing, they avoided having to re-invent the wheel each generation; and they avoided making mistakes already dealt with and were able to build on existing foundations. Indeed what would be the point in studying mediocre works by lesser luminaries or beginning all thought over from square one every few years, when great books by the wisest people—the great sages of civilization—are readily available?

> The reading of all good books is indeed like a conversation with the noblest men of past centuries who were the authors of them, nay a carefully studied conversation, in which they reveal to us none but the best of their thoughts. (Rene Descartes, *Discourse on Method*)

Through the internal dialectical process found in the great books—the references, discussions, critiques, and responses to the thought of the authors' wise predecessors, a process referred to as the "Great Conversation" by Robert M. Hutchins—we may closely follow the development of the investigations conducted by these wise men into the great ideas they have pondered and about which they have written. This manner of study has always been the normative approach to wisdom in the West.

> Until lately the West has regarded it as self-evident that the road to education lay through great books. No man was educated until he was acquainted with the masterpieces of his tradition. . . . They were the principal instruments of liberal education. . . . The goal toward which Western society moves is the Civilization of the Dialogue. The spirit of Western civilization is the spirit of inquiry. Its dominant element is *Logos*.[1]

No ongoing dialogue comparable in duration or breadth exists in the East. Pope Benedict XVI has mentioned that Western civilization has become the dominant civilization because of its closer correspondence to human nature. In his 2006 Regensburg lecture, he noted that there exists a real analogy between our created reason and God, who is *Logos* (meaning both "reason" and "word"). To abandon reason—and hence the dialogue, which is both reason's natural expression and necessary aid—would be contrary both to the nature of man and of God. This cumulative wisdom of the West is preserved and transmitted in its great music and art, but most particularly in the study of its great books which record the results of three millennia of dialogue, guided by reason, concerning the most profound ideas with which we must all grapple such as existence, life, love, happiness, and so forth.

---

[1] Robert M. Hutchins, *The Great Conversation: The Substance of a Liberal Education,* vol. 1, *The Great Books of the Western World* (Chicago: Encyclopedia Brittannica, Inc., 1952).

This manner of learning is greatly facilitated when the reader also engages in a dialectic exchange—a live conversation (in person or now online)—with other readers of the same books, probing and discussing the great ideas contained in them and, one hopes, carrying them a few steps further. This method of learning is often referred to as the Socratic method, after the ancient Athenian philosopher Socrates, who initiated its use as a deliberate way to obtain understanding and wisdom through mutual inquiry and discussion. This same "questioning" method was used by Christ, who often answered questions with other questions, parables, and stories that left the hearers wondering, questioning, and thinking. He already knew the answers, as Socrates often did. The goal was not merely indoctrination of the memory with information, facts, and knowledge, but mind- and life-changing understanding and wisdom.

This study guide is intended for students (if one is still learning, one is a student) who have read—extensively—lesser works, particularly the classic children's literature. Given that degree of preparation, students of high school age and older, including adults, can pick up Homer's *Iliad* and *Odyssey* or Herodotus' *Histories* and other great works and enter into the seminal thought of the most influential books of our culture and civilization. There is reason not to delay such education.

The great books are, for the most part, the most interesting and well written of all books. They were not written for experts. Their wide and enduring appeal to generation after generation testifies to that fact. Readers reasonably prepared for them will find them captivating, entertaining, and enlightening. Naturally, some readers will profit more than others from the great books, but all will profit from learning about the Trojan War, ancient civilizations, the heroes of ancient Greece, the early tragedies, and the thought of Aristotle. Works such as Genesis, the *Aeneid*, Saint Augustine's *Confessions*, Chaucer's *Canterbury Tales*, Dante's *Divine Comedy*, Saint Thomas Aquinas' *Summa theologica*, and Shakespeare's plays are foundational for and/or profoundly influential on our way of life. These works are essential for participation in the Great Conversation mentioned above. The enduring intellectual dialogue begins with the works of Homer, the "father of civilization", and proceeds through the centuries, eventually absorbing the Old and New Testaments in a lengthy reformulation of classical civilization into Western civilization, which continues—albeit always under assault by various errors—right up to our time.

The principal guides in selecting the works of enduring appeal to be included in the corpus of great books, besides generations of readers, include the late, great Dr. Mortimer J. Adler, who worked for eighty years (from 1921 to 2000, when I had the privilege to participate in his last Socratic discussion groups) to restore and keep the great classics, including particularly those by Plato, Aristotle, and Aquinas, in the Western canon of great books. As Dr. Adler put it, "The great books constitute the backbone of a liberal education." But read alone in our postmodernist context of radical skepticism, the great books can easily be misunderstood and used for all manner of mischief. It was precisely a desire to provide a deeper understanding of the importance and influence of the great books—to highlight what is true and great in them and to expose and defang what is false—that inspired Ignatius Press to initiate its important Critical Editions series.

Augmenting the work of Dr. Adler, on behalf of Ignatius Press, is Joseph Pearce, the author of several critically acclaimed, best-selling biographies of great authors, who has diligently worked as the author and/or editor of these study guides to accompany the Ignatius Critical Editions, of which he is also the series editor. Our gratitude extends to Father Joseph Fessio for his encouragement of this much-needed project, which is so broad in scope and vision as to be potentially revolutionary in the schools, colleges, and universities dominated by relativism. Homeschoolers, though somewhat shielded from the relativism of the schools, will find in these guides a welcome and trustworthy means of introduction to the great books and to their careful and critical reading.

Finally, it is worth emphasizing that these Ignatius Critical Editions Study Guides are merely introductory guides with tests, questions, and answer keys helpful for student assessment. The great books themselves are the primary texts, their authors our primary teachers.

Patrick S. J. Carmack
January 18, 2008

Patrick S. J. Carmack, J.D., is the president of the Great Books Academy Homeschool Program (greatbooksacademy.org), the Angelicum Academy Homeschool Program (angelicum.net), the Western Civilization Foundation, and the online publication *Classical Homeschooling Magazine* (classicalhomeschooling.com).

Notes

How to Use This Guide

The Ignatius Critical Editions (ICE) Study Guides are intended to assist students and teachers in their reading of the Ignatius Critical Editions. Each guide gives a short introductory appraisal of the contextual factors surrounding the writing of the literary work, a short "bare bones" summary of the plot, and a more in-depth summary of some of the essential critical aspects of the work. There is also a list of things to think about while reading the book, designed to focus the reader's critical faculties. These points to ponder will enable the reader to rise above a merely recreational reading of the text to a level of critical and literary appreciation befitting the work itself.

Finally, there are questions for the student to answer. These fall into two distinct categories: questions concerned with a knowledge of the *facts* of the work, and questions concerned with analyzing the *truths* that emerge from the work. This approach is rooted in the fundamental axiom, taught by great philosophers such as Aristotle and Saint Thomas Aquinas, that we must go *through* the facts *to* the truth. Put simply, an inadequate knowledge of the facts of a work (who did what and when, who said what to whom, etc.) will inevitably lead to a failure to understand the work on its deeper levels of meaning.

As such, readers of the work are strongly encouraged to answer all the *fact-related* questions in part 1. The close reading of the text that this will entail will prepare them for the essay questions in part 2. With regard to the latter, it is left to the discretion of the teacher (or the reader) as to how many of these questions should be answered. Some of the questions, particularly those calling for a contextual reading of the work in relation to other works, might be unsuitable for less-advanced students or readers. In such cases, the teacher (or reader) should use his discretion in deciding which of the essay questions should be answered. In any event, you have been provided with an abundance of questions from which to choose!

Teachers should also be aware that the answer key can be removed before the study guide is made available to the student. Answers to the questions in the "Bare Bones" and "Things to Think About" sections are not included in the answer key because these questions are intended to raise issues for the student to ponder and are not intended to be employed for examination purposes.

It should be noted that the Ignatius Critical Editions and the ICE Study Guides approach these great works of literature from a tradition-oriented perspective. Those seeking deconstruction, "queer theory", feminism, postcolonialism, and other manifestations of the latest academic fads and fashions will be disappointed. If you are unable to think outside the postmodern box, this guide is not for you!

Context

Shakespeare's primary literary source for the tale of *Macbeth* was Raphael Holinshed's popular history the *Chronicles of England, Scotlande and Irelande*, published in 1577. Holinshed's version of the story relied heavily on Hector Boece's *Scotorum historiae* (1527). In the crafting of the witches and other supernatural elements in the play, Shakespeare may also have referred to King James I's 1599 work on witchcraft, *Daemonologie*. He may also have drawn from the alleged attempted assassination of King James (then of Scotland, and not yet of England) in 1600 by the brother of the Earl of Gowrie. In that case, Shakespeare may have been influenced by a controversial play, written by one of his theatrical colleagues, entitled *The Tragedy of Gowrie* (1604).

The use of Holinshed's *Chronicles*, which was a favored source for the Bard, is not in itself significant but rather provides a fascinating counterpoint for examining Shakespeare's modifications to the original story. Of particular note is a marked alteration of the character of Banquo, who in Holinshed's version is an accomplice to the murder of Duncan. In understanding this change, the fact that Banquo was believed to be an ancestor of the reigning king, James I of England and VI of Scotland, is illuminative. In fact, the shadow of the newly crowned king can be seen in many aspects of the play, beginning with the dating of the text.

The actual date of the composition of *Macbeth* is uncertain but is conjectured to fall somewhere between 1603 and 1606, the early years of the reign of King James I. The text itself displays many elements indicative of a 1606 completion, particularly in possible allusions to the Gunpowder Plot of 1605. A performance of the play is first recorded in 1611, and it first appeared in print in the First Folio, published in 1623, which is the only source for Shakespeare's text.

James VI of Scotland (1566–1625), who inherited the Scottish throne as a baby, succeeded to the throne of England in 1603 when Elizabeth I (1533–1603) died without issue. Historians have often viewed his reign as a time when the arts flourished—a "golden age" of literature and drama, continuing the sumptuous pageantry and imaginatively rich Elizabethan age. It is true that a host of talented poets and playwrights produced remarkable works during both the Elizabethan and the Jacobean period; however, both reigns were very much defined by oppressive governmental controls and fierce religious persecution. It was hoped that much of the unrest suffered under Elizabeth, who drew her monarchical strength from a Machiavellian philosophy, would be alleviated under James, and, indeed, the early months of his reign seemed to promise blessed relief to the beleaguered Catholic community. The return of fierce persecution would cast a dark shadow over the literary world, over Catholics and Protestants alike, and it is perhaps this dark shadow that broods ominously over the action of this darkest of Shakespeare's plays.

Bare Bones: The Skeleton Plot

The play begins with the brief entrance of three witches, who chant and call upon their familiars.

In the second scene, Duncan, the king of Scotland, along with a circle of Scottish thanes and royal attendants, receives the news of victory in a battle against a rebel named Macdonwald who has allied with the Norwegian king. As the captain gives his report, the prowess of the "brave Macbeth" is highly lauded (1.2.16). Macbeth and Banquo are the redoubtable heroes of the field. Particular description is given of Macbeth's triumph over the traitorous Thane of Cawdor. As a reward, Duncan confers the title of Thane of Cawdor on Macbeth.

The three witches reappear in the third scene, speaking the words of a charm in anticipation of the appearance of Macbeth. Macbeth and Banquo are startled to see the three witches—"[s]o wither'd, and so wild in their attire"—and are bewildered but fascinated by the prophetic statements that fall from their lips (1.3.40). They greet Macbeth as "Thane of Glamis" (his current title), "Thane of Cawdor", and "King hereafter". When Banquo addresses them, they call him "[l]esser than Macbeth, and greater / Not so happy, yet much happier", and tell him: "Thou shalt get kings, though thou be none" (1.3.67). Macbeth presses the witches for an explanation of their mysterious sayings, but they vanish, leaving the two men perplexed. They are not left to wonder long; they are joined by their fellow thanes, Ross and Angus, and are soon informed of Duncan's delight in their victory, and particularly of the conferment of the title of Thane of Cawdor on Macbeth. Banquo and

Macbeth wonder anew and, in an aside, Macbeth expresses the breadth of his astonishment. The three witches greeted him as Thane of Glamis, which indeed he was, and as Thane of Cawdor, which he has now become. From this he begins to speculate whether these two fulfillments are "happy prologues to the swelling act / Of the imperial theme" (1.3.128–29). As he begins to covet the throne, murder is mentioned for the first time in the play, though it "is but fantastical" (1.3.139). Turning from his reverie, Macbeth urges Banquo to think over this encounter with the witches so that they might discuss it between themselves later.

In the fourth scene, Macbeth and Banquo join the king and his attendants. Duncan expresses his gratitude and admiration for the two captains, and in return Macbeth and Banquo declare their allegiance to and affection for him. Duncan settles his estate on his eldest son, Malcolm, and names him Prince of Cumberland, the heir to the Scottish throne. Duncan then announces his plan of visiting Macbeth at the castle at Inverness, and Macbeth hurries away to tell his wife of the royal approach. In Macbeth's absence, Duncan once again speaks highly of his loyal thane, calling Macbeth "a peerless kinsman" (1.4.58).

Meanwhile, in the fifth scene, Lady Macbeth reads a letter from her husband in which he acquaints her with the victory, his encounter with the witches, and the subsequent fulfillment of their prophecy regarding Cawdor. She is expressively excited by what she reads and declares at the conclusion of the letter that Macbeth "shalt be / What thou art promis'd" (1.5.12–13). That her mind already runs to murder is soon apparent, as she expresses concern that her husband is "too full o' th' milk of human kindness / To catch the nearest way" (i.e., killing Duncan and usurping the throne) (1.5.13–14). Hearing that Macbeth is even now arriving at the castle, Lady Macbeth calls upon "you spirits / That tend on mortal thoughts" (1.5.37–38) to prepare her for a murderous task. When her husband enters, she greets him by his titles and, as he announces the king's approach that night, immediately begins to allude to murder and presses the urgency of this "night's great business" (1.5.65). Macbeth dismisses the subject to be discussed later, but she concludes the scene with a sense of assured purpose.

In the brief sixth scene, Duncan, Malcolm, Donalbain, Banquo, Lennox, Macduff, Ross, Angus, and the king's attendants arrive at the castle. Duncan exchanges gracious words of affection with his host and hostess.

The night comes in the seventh scene and shows Macbeth tortured with indecision. He fears both judgment and discovery. In particular he ponders his place as host, with his loyalty sworn to the king. He concludes with a fierce desire for haste: "If it were done when 'tis done, then 'twere well / It were done quickly" (1.7.1–2). Lady Macbeth appears at her lord's side and chides him as a "coward" (1.7.43). To his expressions of concern that their plan might fail, she scornfully replies by urging him to "screw [his] courage to the sticking place" and be resolved (1.7.60). Macbeth commends her "undaunted mettle" and declares his resolve renewed (1.7.73); the murder will be committed that night. Meanwhile, husband and wife go to continue their false performance as gracious hosts toward their victim.

Act 2 begins with Banquo and his son, Fleance. Banquo confesses himself sleepy but fears the "cursed thoughts that nature / Gives way to in repose" (2.1.8–9). His mind runs much on the encounter with the witches. He is plagued with vague fears, so that when Macbeth and a servant appear, Banquo is startled at their arrival and, before he recognizes them, draws his sword. Macbeth identifies himself as "[a] friend" (2.1.11), and, recognizing his host, Banquo speaks with him briefly, referring to the meeting with the Weird Sisters. When Banquo and Fleance leave for sleep, Macbeth sends his servant away. Left alone, Macbeth is haunted by an invisible dagger (the presence of which is conveyed by Macbeth's uttering the words: "Is this a dagger which I see before me . . . ?" [2.1.33]) covered in blood. All things speak to him of the murder he is about to commit—the night itself, the howling of wolves in the distance, and the influence of witchcraft. When he hears a bell rung by his wife—their planned signal—he goes to commit the murder of Duncan. "Hear it not, Duncan," he cries, "for it is a knell / That summons thee to heaven or to hell" (2.1.63–64).

The second scene opens with the entrance of Lady Macbeth, who is full of boldness and eagerness, awaiting news of her husband's murderous deed. Like Macbeth, she is startled by noises, but she is untroubled by guilt or scruples. She has drugged the two grooms attending on Duncan and laid their daggers nearby for her husband's murderous use. Macbeth cries out: "Who's there! What, ho!" (2.2.8), and she fears that he has been forestalled and that Duncan has not been killed. She adds to herself that, had Duncan "not resembled / My father as he slept, I had done't" (2.2.12–13). Macbeth appears and announces that he has killed Duncan. Overwrought by the deed he has committed, he starts in alarm at noises in the night, shows his wife his bloody hands, and speaks hauntingly of the murder. When he hears a guest cry out in sleep: "God bless us", Macbeth finds himself unable to say "Amen" in response (2.2.29, 31). This incapacity preoccupies his overexcited mind, though his wife urges him not to think of the deed now that it is committed, declaring that such brooding "will make us mad" (2.2.34).

Macbeth's wildness increases until his wife stops him, takes the bloody daggers from his hands, and goes to mark the grooms with the blood so that they will be taken for the murderers. Left alone, Macbeth wonders in horror: "Will all great Neptune's ocean wash this blood / Clean from my hand?" (2.2.60–61). Lady Macbeth returns with bloody hands and insists: "A little water clears us of this deed" (2.2.67). Macbeth is so overwrought that he even wishes aloud that Duncan could be awakened.

Scene 3 opens upon an old porter who receives the thanes Macduff and Lennox at the gate. They are soon joined by their host, Macbeth. Macduff goes in to see the king, leaving Lennox and Macbeth together. After Lennox speaks of the "unruly" behavior of the night before, which was full of dark, foreboding occurrences, Macduff hurries back with the horrifying news of Duncan's murder (2.3.65–67). While Macbeth and Lennox run to the king's chambers, Macduff raises the alarm bell. Lady Macbeth comes and challenges Macduff for making so much noise; she expresses horror at the news when he tells her of the murder of Duncan. Soon the entire house is in an uproar. Malcolm and Donalbain appear and are informed of their father's death. The grooms, implicated in the crime, have been killed by Macbeth in a "fury" (2.3.105). When Macbeth is questioned regarding this rash deed, he defends himself as being in a passion, overwhelmed by the horror of Duncan's death. Immediately following, Lady Macbeth faints. Malcolm and Donalbain suspect that something more is afoot and determine to discuss the matter privately together. When the other men go to dress and to consider the matter at hand, the two sons of Duncan express their doubts and their fears; they fear that their father died treacherously and that his murderer will seek to murder them as well, thereby clearing a path to the throne. They determine therefore to flee.

Scene 4 opens with Ross speaking to an old man who describes all of the strange happenings of the night of the murder. Macduff comes and speaks with Ross. The two dead grooms have indeed been taken for the murderers, hired (it is believed) by Malcolm and Donalbain, whose flight has been generally taken as an indication of their guilt. Meanwhile, Macbeth has been named king and has "gone to Scone / To be invested" (2.4.31–32). Ross determines to go to Scone to see Macbeth crowned, but Macduff decides to return to his home of Fife. They both leave with the blessing of the old man.

Act 3 begins with Banquo meditating on the fulfillment of the witches' prophecies with regard to Macbeth. He fears that the new king "play'dst most foully for't" and muses further regarding the prophecy alluding to himself and his sons: "that myself should be the root and father / Of many kings" (3.1.3, 5–6). His reverie is interrupted by the entrance of Macbeth, Lady Macbeth, and their court, now housed in the castle at Forres. The matter now weighing on Macbeth's mind is the flight of Malcolm and Donalbain, who are in England and Ireland, asserting their innocence in the death of their father and instead "filling their hearers / With strange invention" (3.1.31–32). Banquo departs on a brief trip, and the rest of the court leaves, except for the newly crowned king. Macbeth broods over his "fears in Banquo" (3.1.48). He recalls how the witches hailed Banquo as the "father to a line of kings" while giving Macbeth "a fruitless crown" and a "[b]arren sceptre in [his] gripe" (3.1.59–61). Now he feels betrayed, as if he has killed Duncan to serve Banquo's issue: "To make them kings—the seeds of Banquo kings!" (3.1.69). His servant reenters with two murderers, both of whom have deep-seated grudges against Banquo and are eager for revenge. Linking his own motivations to theirs, Macbeth commissions them to murder Banquo and Banquo's son, Fleance, thereby routing the threat of the line of Banquo.

At the opening of scene 2, Lady Macbeth lectures her husband for keeping alone and worrying over "sorriest fancies" when "[w]hat's done is done" (3.2.9, 12). Macbeth alludes to his concerns regarding Banquo and hints darkly at some solution to the problem: "[T]here shall be done / A deed of dreadful note" (3.2.43–44). When Lady Macbeth presses to know what will be done, he tells her: "Be innocent of the knowledge" (3.2.45).

Scene 3 presents the murder of Banquo in the forest near the palace at Forres. While awaiting their victim in the woods, the two murderers are joined by a third murderer. Banquo and Fleance enter and are attacked. Banquo is struck down and dies, crying out for his son to flee so that he can avenge his father's death. Fleance escapes.

Scene 4 returns to the palace at Forres. Macbeth, Lady Macbeth, and their thanes attend a banquet. Before their feast commences, the first murderer comes to speak with Macbeth, who rises to learn of the fate of Banquo and the escape of Fleance. With the knowledge that Fleance is still alive, Macbeth is overcome with a "fit" of shivering: "[N]ow I am cabin'd, cribb'd, confin'd, bound in / To saucy doubts and fears" (3.4.24–25). The murder of Banquo has not freed him from the dangers implicit in the witches' prophecies. He returns to the feast, where Lady Macbeth chides him for dampening the spirits of his guests by his strange and brooding behavior. Meanwhile, the ghost of Banquo enters and sits at Macbeth's place. Macbeth readies himself to be lord over the table and becomes regally jovial. He is urged to sit but notes that all the seats are filled. When he is gestured toward the empty chair (which contains Banquo's ghost), Macbeth reacts with horror at the sight, to the astonishment and perplexity of his fellows, and immediately begins professing his innocence of Banquo's death. Lady Macbeth tries to convince the bewildered guests that her husband is merely suffering from a vague malady that has occasionally afflicted him since he was a child. Meanwhile, she tries to compel her husband to be "a man" and to control his strange behavior (3.4.58). When Macbeth tries to defend himself, describing the ghostly apparition, Lady Macbeth scoffs at him. The ghost departs, and Macbeth endeavors to rally himself and to beg his friends' pardon for his "strange infirmity" (3.4.86). Macbeth makes a toast, and they all eagerly pledge with him, but the ghost returns and Macbeth is once more unmanned at the sight. The guests all leave. When Macbeth is alone with his wife, he tells her, with haunting insistence: "It will have blood; they say blood will have blood" (3.4.122). Then he questions her regarding the absence of Macduff. He determines to visit the Weird Sisters and to ask them about this absent thane. Lady Macbeth declares that he is in need of "the season of all natures, sleep" (3.4.141).

Scene 5 returns to the heath. The three witches cavort and cackle with Hecate, the goddess of witchcraft.

In scene 6, in the palace at Forres, Lennox and another lord discuss the recent events, including the death of Banquo, the flight of Fleance, and Macduff's refusal to attend on Macbeth.

They openly consider the dangers of the times and the growing tyranny of Macbeth, acknowledging him as the "hand accurs'd" ruling over Scotland (3.6.49). They conclude by entertaining the idea of sending to England to try and bring back Malcolm to reclaim the throne usurped from his father.

The first scene of act 4 takes place in a dark cave with the three witches presiding over a boiling cauldron. One of the witches announces the approach of Macbeth: "By the pricking of my thumbs, / Something wicked this way comes" (4.1.44–45). He inquires as to their business, and they declare that they do a "deed without a name" (i.e., witchcraft) (4.1.49).

At Macbeth's command, they call up three apparitions. The first apparition warns Macbeth: "Beware Macduff; / Beware the Thane of Fife" (4.1.72–73). The second apparition, a bloody child, declares that "none of woman born / Shall harm Macbeth" (4.1.80–81). The third apparition, a child crowned with a tree in his hand, pronounces that Macbeth will not be vanquished until "[g]reat Birnam wood to high Dunsinane Hill / Shall come against him" (4.1.93–94). Macbeth is overjoyed at the apparent assurances of invincibility, but anxiety still lingers, so he presses to know whether the prophecy regarding the kingship and Banquo's line is true. The witches urge him to "[s]eek to know no more" (4.1.103), but at his insistence a vision arises of eight kings and Banquo, with the last king holding a mirror in his hand. To Macbeth's horror, the mirror reflects a seemingly endless royal line, beginning with Banquo. The witches dance an antic round and disappear, leaving Macbeth in anxiety and frustration, cursing the hour. When Lennox appears and informs him that Macduff has fled to England, Macbeth heeds the warning from the first apparition and orders that the castle at Fife be attacked and the entire family of Macduff killed.

The second scene opens upon Lady Macduff and her son, visited in Fife by Ross. Lady Macduff is distressed and horrified over her husband's flight, fearing he has behaved traitorously and deserted his family. After Ross departs, a messenger comes and tells Lady Macduff that danger is upon them. The murderers enter and kill the son of Macduff. Lady Macduff runs from the stage, screaming: "Murder!"

In the third scene, Macduff and Malcolm meet in England. Macduff urges Malcolm to return to Scotland and take up arms against Macbeth. To test the virtue of the Thane of Fife, Malcolm begins to attribute a host of vices to himself. When Macduff, convinced that Malcolm is indeed full of vice, laments the loss of a goodly king and even says that a man so vicious is not fit "to live" (4.3.103), Malcolm then reveals that his words were designed to test Macduff's loyalty. They speak briefly of the sanctity of the king of England, Edward the Confessor, who cures the sick through his divine touch. Ross joins them and informs Macduff of the slaughter of his family. The grief and rage of Macduff waxes hot, and the men begin to make preparations to return to Scotland and rout the tyrant from the throne.

The fifth act begins in the castle at Dunsinane. A doctor of physic confers with a waiting-gentlewoman regarding Lady Macbeth, who has been sleepwalking and speaking of strange things in her sleep. While they are standing together, they witness Lady Macbeth, who is haunted by the death of Duncan and continuously rubs her hands in an effort to remove the blood, crying: "Out, damned spot! out, I say!" (5.1.33). She murmurs with sad horror: "[W]ho would have thought the old man to have had so much blood in him?" (5.1.36–38). In the midst of her dream, she addresses her husband and runs on in her speech with mad urgency. The doctor is deeply disturbed and dreads to believe the suspicions planted by what he has seen and heard.

In scene 2, the thanes loyal to Malcolm join Macduff in the country near Dunsinane. They discuss the rumors that Macbeth has become mad. They then announce their plan to meet with Malcolm and the rest of their army at Birnam Wood.

Scene 3 briefly presents Macbeth, the doctor, and Macbeth's attendants. Macbeth reacts with fury to reports of the strength of the rebels and refers with swaggering assurance to the apparitions he witnessed in the cave with the three witches. He arms himself, responding angrily to the news of the army now marching against him.

Malcolm's army comes together in scene 4. As they stand before Birnam Wood, Malcolm orders every soldier to cut off a piece of a bough and carry it before him, thereby concealing the true size of their army.

In scene 5, preparations for battle continue in the castle at Dunsinane. Macbeth hears the cry of women and learns of the death of his wife. He declares that she "should have died hereafter" (5.5.17). Then, in a dark, despairing soliloquy, he asserts:

> Life's but a walking shadow, a poor player,
> That struts and frets his hour upon the stage,
> And then is heard no more; it is a tale
> Told by an idiot, full of sound and fury,
> Signifying nothing. (5.5.24–28)

He becomes increasingly reckless in his preparations for the battle, declaring his decreasing care whether he lives or dies. When, however, he hears of the seeming approach of Birnam Wood, he is overcome with horror.

Scene 6 briefly presents the arrival of the army before the castle of Dunsinane. Malcolm orders his men to their places; then they all throw down their branches, and the host is revealed.

In scene 7, Macbeth fights with and kills young Siward. Macduff enters, eager to find Macbeth and calling out for revenge for the death of his family.

The battle continues into scene 8. Speaking aloud in the midst of the field, Macbeth refuses to take the way of "the Roman fool" by killing himself (5.8.1) and announces his determination to kill as many of his adversaries as he can before being slain. Macduff appears, declaring his intention of killing the "hell-hound" who slew his family (5.8.3). Macbeth rejects the threat, asserting that it would be impossible to kill him, and recites the prophecy as his proof. Macduff's response strikes terror into Macbeth's heart:

> Despair thy charm;
> And let the angel whom thou still hast serv'd
> Tell thee Macduff was from his mother's womb
> Untimely ripp'd. (5.8.14–16)

With this revelation of the misleading nature of the prophecy, Macbeth despairs. When Macduff orders him to fight on or to yield, Macbeth refuses to yield and their battle continues offstage. Meanwhile, a retreat is sounded. Malcolm comes forward with his men and is met by Macduff, who bears the decapitated head of Macbeth. Malcolm is declared king and leaves with his loyal thanes to be crowned at Scone.

Notes

Words Made Flesh: Summary of Critical Appraisals and Study Questions

The questions posed in this section are not intended for examination purposes but are designed to prompt appropriate trains of thought for the student to ponder as he reads the work. Questions intended for examination purposes are to be found in the "Study Questions on the Text" at the end of the study guide.

Joseph Pearce: "*Macbeth*: An Introduction"

The historical backdrop upon which the "tragedy of errors" of *Macbeth* operates brings with it great darkness. In particular the Gunpowder Plot (1605), the rule of James I, and consequent questions of the role of the monarchy and of Christianity and Machiavellianism persist. Shakespeare's work in the end presents a defense of the monarchy but with the understanding that the king is subservient to Christian moral precepts. This notion of a monarch who is not, in and of himself, omnipotent and infallible but rather is obliged to follow the dictates of the moral law strikes at the heart of both the Elizabethan and the Jacobean struggle. The question that is asked is: Will a king be a virtuous monarch or will he ally himself with evil for the sake of a perceived good? The totalitarian control of Queen Elizabeth I was followed by the equally complex system of governmental control under King James I. Shakespeare, who had hoped to find under the new king a mitigation of religious persecution, witnessed instead a renewal of the intensity of governmental suppressions.

Consequently, *Macbeth* is fraught with the darkness of disappointment, even as it is full of the presence of supernatural evil. The perversion of a man and his subsequent descent into the darkness of sin is its theme. Through the characters of Macbeth and his wife, the playwright confronts the essence of Machiavellian reasoning, demanding whether ostensibly good ends can be pursued through evil means. At the same time, the play confronts tyranny and the web of falsehood that supports it. Is man a slave to his fate, the play asks, a victim of supernatural forces? Or does he bring about his own fate through his actions? Macbeth, blinded by ambition, loses his moral compass, becoming a slave to his own ego. With the loss of God, the sinful man becomes the center of his own universe. Macbeth's solipsism ends poignantly in tormented "nothing", and even in the loss of his humanity; as Chesterton put it, Macbeth at the end of the play "is not merely a wild beast; he is a caged wild beast."

1. Consider the proposed relation between *Macbeth* and Jacobean anti-Catholicism, particularly with regard to the Gunpowder Plot. Do you agree with Pearce's historical hypothesis?

2. Is the "supernatural superstructure" of the play really as evident as Pearce suggests? What is the relationship between the more fantastical elements of the play (i.e., witchcraft and the attendant apparitions) and the questions of morality and the human soul?

3. If Macbeth indeed becomes prey of his "sin-deceived ego", is there a place for the redemption of the human ego in the midst of the play's dark conclusion?

James Bemis: "*Macbeth* on Film"

Modernity's fascination with *Macbeth* has been demonstrated by the at least forty-seven filmed adaptations and the frequency with which the play is staged. However, the real crux of *Macbeth* directly opposes the tenets of modernity: the destruction of a soul by demonic forces is not a subject countenanced by modern secularism; further, the play's condemnation of the sins of Macbeth and Lady Macbeth is completely antithetical to modernity's rejection of the notion of sin. As the presence of the supernatural and the belief in the immorality of the human soul are both dismissed by secular modernity, the very framework of the play and the underlying reasoning inherent in its plot are stumbling blocks to a modern director.

The representation of Macbeth and Lady Macbeth must be at the heart of any adaptation, and examination of certain key scenes (seven for the former character and three for the latter) provides the pertinent tools for making a critical judgment of any given film. Bemis addresses five major films: the 1948 production by Orson Welles at Republic Pictures, Hugh Hefner's collaboration with Roman Polanski through Playboy Productions (1970), a Royal Shakespeare Company performance (1979), the BBC and Time Life Films production of 1983, and the 2006 work produced by Film Finance Corporation Australia. Bemis' analysis and review of these five film adaptations show the predictable result: the loss of God that brings Macbeth to despair and death renders impossible a full and appreciative representation of such a tale in a society that rejects God. Consequently, the failure of these films in realizing the full spiritual weight of *Macbeth* undermines their effectiveness as adaptations and is at the same time indicative of the despair and death rampant in the society that created them.

1. Have you seen any of the films discussed by Bemis? If so, do you agree with his evaluation?

2. Taking into consideration all of the problematic elements of these films, what worth can be found in the adaptation of *Macbeth* from the stage to film? Are the atmospherics of the play too tempting to the filmmaker to allow a properly deep presentation of the heart of the play?

3. Do you agree with Bemis' final judgment of modern society in the light of these films? If not, how would you modify his assessment?

Robert Carballo: "'Fair is foul, and foul is fair': *Macbeth* as Morality Play and Discreet Exemplum"

The philosophical underpinnings of *Macbeth*, coherent though somewhat shrouded in overt theatricality, draw heavily from the Greek (via the medieval) tradition of the morality play and the exemplum. The moral atmosphere and vision of the Catholic European Middle Ages is clearly shown throughout the play, especially in its dramatization of the complexities of human moral action. *Macbeth* in essence presents traditional Christian morality in contrast to the growing influences of Machiavellianism and Renaissance secularism.

The older tradition that underlies *Macbeth* challenges the modern conceptions of governance and power, of human nature and the consequences of sin, and of virtue and vice, particularly with regard to men in authority. *Macbeth*, in the midst of its sensationalized atmospherics and rapid pacing, presents a penetrating statement on human nature and the consequences of evil in high places. It provides a moral evaluation on both a societal scale (with regard to the monarchy) and even more dramatically on the scale of the individual soul, with profound moral and psychological insight. The soul of Macbeth faces worldly temptations against truth and justice. Part morality play and part exemplum, *Macbeth* essentially represents the transition from medieval Christianity, with its holistic appreciation of the human person and of society as a whole, to nascent secular modernity. The concluding message is one that surely speaks clearly to the reader of today.

1. Explain the difference between a morality tale and an exemplum, and consider *Macbeth* in the light of both terms.

2. What are the elements of weakness in the conscience of Macbeth? What should be the proper role of conscience in the moral life of man or of a society? How would this revitalized conscience work in the face of the modern temptations to which Macbeth falls prey?

3. How does Carballo characterize Lady Macbeth? Is her character redeemable or irredeemable?

Hildegard Hammerschmidt-Hummel: "*The Tragedy of Macbeth*: A History Play with a Message for Shakespeare's Contemporaries?"

The indicators that have led scholars to date the composition of *Macbeth* after the Gunpowder Plot (1605) and the trial of the superior of the English Jesuits Henry Garnet (1606), when more fully considered in the light of Shakespeare's sources and the effects of governmentally imposed anti-Catholic persecution, indicate further that *Macbeth* fulfills all but one of the established criteria for Elizabethan history plays. In particular, Shakespeare's use and embellishment of his sources demonstrates the pertinence of the play's events to the time in which the author lived. His decision to distance his work from the present time by setting it in the medieval history of Scotland allows Shakespeare to address the subject of Jacobean England, specifically with regard to the oppression of Catholic subjects under James I.

The complexities of his modifications of earlier sources, along with the precise intricacies of the text itself, unite (though in mosaic form) to create a compelling message to Shakespeare's contemporaries concerning the hidden story of persecuted Catholics. This discernable recusant narrative sheds an interesting light on the character of Shakespeare himself and on his attitudes toward major events such as the Gunpowder Plot.

1. Is Hammerschmidt-Hummel's case for the dating of *Macbeth* after the Gunpowder Plot convincing?

2. In what ways do the pressures and prejudices of anti-Catholicism play out across *Macbeth*?

3. Contrast Hammerschmidt-Hummel's article with the representations of the Elizabethan and Jacobean religious struggle provided by Pearce and, indirectly, by Carballo.

Regis Martin: "Depraved or Determined? *Macbeth* and the Problem of Free Will"

The moral message of the play, at its starkest and simplest, emphatically asserts the Fifth Commandment: Thou shalt not kill. Macbeth's descent into sin and despair exposes the slope of sin toward evil itself. However, in the light of the play's emphasis on the agency of supernatural evil, particularly as represented by witchcraft, the question of Macbeth's own moral agency, his free will, must be considered. The prophecies and apparitions regarding his fate seem to imply that he has no course except for that mapped out for him by the three witches, servants of Satan.

The question therefore becomes: Is Macbeth a victim? Assuredly not. His descent toward nihilism is clearly accomplished through use of his human liberty. Indeed, for the play even to be morally consequent—not to mention humanly compelling—evil must operate within the paradigm of man's free will. In essence, the tragedy of the play relies on the operation of Macbeth's freedom. In the end, even the supernatural evil in which Macbeth has put his faith disappears, leaving him with the predictable results of sin: despair, loneliness, desolation. The fruits of nihilism are his: he is a man without grace, without God.

1. What do the "accumulating weirdness" of *Macbeth* and the "starkest simplicity" of its moral message work together to accomplish in the play?

2. According to Martin, can the notions of fate or fortune and of free will exist simultaneously with each other? Are they in conflict or confused in *Macbeth*?

3. How does Macbeth's sin bring him to atheistic nihilism?

Lee Oser: "The Vision of Evil in *Macbeth*"

The representation of evil in *Macbeth* encompasses a complex spectrum, from its supernatural representation in the witches to the weakness and sin inherent in Banquo's conforming to the reign of Macbeth, in spite of his reason and his proper loyalties. Shakespeare's Christianity and scepticism produce a nuanced understanding of belief, but at its heart lies an understanding of the human soul where its destiny is taken seriously. Certain quasi-religious convictions—the existence of the soul, the existence of a natural order, and the existence of evil—are foundational to Shakespeare's work.

Macbeth is possessed of a free will, reason, a conscience, and corporeality. These work together holistically and within the context of the larger societal framework. In the descent of a single soul toward evil, the holistic structure crumbles, even to the point of threatening the stability of the larger framework. Evil attacks human nature by attacking man's reason; thus Macbeth is led to rash action, disordering his reason and rendering deeply fallible his conscience. The results can be seen throughout the play, and in a distinct way through Macbeth's relationship with Lady Macbeth and their shared corporeality as husband and wife. The conclusion of the play, though demonstrating the final punishment of sin, is not jubilant but rather poignant as it gestures toward man's concupiscence, which can draw him toward evil in spite of his natural inclination toward the good.

1. In Holinshed's *Chronicles*, Banquo was Macbeth's coconspirator. How does Oser's discussion of the "sins" of Banquo reflect on Shakespeare's change of the character?

2. Consider Oser's argument concerning the scepticism of Shakespeare in the light of other critical assessments of the religiosity of both the playwright and his play. (See the articles by Hammerschmidt-Hummel, Pearce, and Carballo.)

3. What is Macbeth's "dark epiphany"? What does it reflect when juxtaposed with the heroism of Macduff?

Things to Think About
While Reading the Play

The questions posed in this section are not intended for examination purposes but are designed to prompt appropriate trains of thought for the student to ponder as he reads the work. Questions intended for examination purposes are to be found in the "Study Questions on the Text" at the end of the study guide.

1. Consider the rapidity with which the action of the play moves, both in the light of the fact that the only authoritative version is of rather late date (1623) and in the light of the plot trajectory (i.e., the descent of a human soul through sin). How does the speed of the play serve the sense of moral urgency? Is there another significance to be found in the pervasive rapidity, both of the dramatic action and with regard to the making of decisions?

2. The first act is fraught with moments where characters express their affection or swear their fealty to one another—particularly by the thanes with reference to Duncan, and by the king toward his "loyal" thanes. Follow the course of all such bonds and be particularly attentive to changing definitions of "love" and "loyalty".

3. From this consideration of love and loyalty and the bonds forged by them, move to meditate on the relationship between

familial order and social order, particularly within a monarchical society. What are the effects of internal corruption on the rest of society? In particular, attend to examples of fatherhood and kingship, especially Duncan, Macbeth, and Macduff. Also consider this subject in the light of the larger historical context (i.e., the divine right of kings and Machiavellianism, particularly with regard to the reign of James I and, retrospectively, the reign of Elizabeth I).

4. Manifestations of the supernatural are vividly—and even ostentatiously—displayed throughout the play. Consider the visible and the invisible, the actual and the perceived, the theatrical and the metaphysical. What are the complexities of evil presented in *Macbeth*, and where is the converse presentation of good? Think carefully about the function of the witches in the plot; are they the primary catalysts to the action of the play? How are they characterized? What other representations of evil can be identified? How do they function in relation to each other?

5. Following on the heels of this consideration of the supernatural, think about the role of fate or fortune, providence, and free will. Macbeth seems driven by the fate described to him through the prophecies and apparitions presented by the three witches; yet he commits moral acts as a man endowed with free will. Is the revelation he seems to receive from these supernatural agents empowering, disempowering, or enabling? How? Think about the theory of the divine right of kings. What does the Jacobean development of this issue signify with regard to this theme in *Macbeth*?

6. Think about courage and ambition in all of the characters, particularly Macbeth, Macduff, Lady Macbeth, and Malcolm. How does Macbeth's military prowess (described in 1.2.16–41) reflect upon his character throughout, espe-

cially in the light of his moral hesitancy regarding murder at early moments in the play? What is the significance of Lady Macbeth's frequent questioning of his courage and even of his manhood? Are courage and ambition fundamentally opposed? What is false fortitude? Are boldness and courage the same thing?

7. Think about the darkness of the play; how much of the action occurs under the cover of night? How much is this a reflection of the interior state of characters? Consider also the different manifestations of blindness—moral blindness to the consequences of actions, blindness to danger, blindness to deceit. What things can be seen? How much is "sight" a demonstration of an inner understanding? What is the relation between the pervasive darkness and Macbeth's emotional and spiritual state at the ending of the play?

Study Questions on the Text
of *Macbeth*

Part One—Knowledge of the Text

1. What new title is Macbeth given after the victory in the battle of Act 1?

2. What do the witches prophesy when they meet Macbeth and Banquo in Act 1?

3. Who first conceives of the murder of Duncan?

4. Who discovers the death of Duncan?

5. "Come, you spirits / That tend on mortal thoughts, unsex me here." Whose words are these?

6. "There's daggers in men's smiles; the near in blood, / The nearer bloody." Whose words are these?

7. Who is convicted of the murder of Duncan?

8. Who commits the "deed without a name"?

9. What are the three apparitions seen by Macbeth in the cave with the three witches? How are these three apparitions fulfilled?

10. Who visits Lady Macduff and speaks with her of her husband's journey to England?

11. What is the name of Macbeth's armorer?

12. "Out, damned spot! out, I say!" Whose words are these?

13. How does Lady Macbeth die?

14. "Out, out, brief candle!" Whose words are these?

15. Who first names Malcolm as king of Scotland?

Part Two—Essay Questions

1. What is the nature of courage? What is the nature of ambition? How are both used throughout the play for different ends?

2. What does Macbeth's military prowess signify for his character? Does the image of him as "Bellona's bridegroom" (1.2.55) develop across the play?

3. What is the nature of the relationship between Macbeth and Lady Macbeth? Directors have frequently presented them in early scenes as an affectionate couple; is this reading an appropriate one? How—if at all—does their relationship change over the course of the play?

4. Consider how rapidly Macbeth and his wife both leap to the option of murder when considering their path to the throne. What does this rapidity in forming the intention and means for murder demonstrate about their characters?

5. What is the function of the occult in *Macbeth*? How is it presented? What is its effect on characters, and in terms of staging, what would its effect possibly be on the audience? How does the presence of the witches work in the context of a possible moral message in the play?

6. Consider the characters of men—such as Banquo and Lennox—who are not at the forefront either of Macbeth's usurpation or of Malcolm's reclamation of the throne. What degrees of moral culpability are there between resistance or defiance and submission or compromise?

7. What is the purpose of the unseen presence of King Edward the Confessor? What does his character demonstrate in terms of an ideal vision of the monarchy? For whom is he a fitting counterpoint?

8. The play concludes with the routing of the tyrant Macbeth and the crowning of Malcolm as king. How does the character of Malcolm measure up to notions of kingship represented throughout the play? Will he be a good king?

9. What is the role of blood in the play, especially in reference to the deaths that occur offstage?

10. Tragedy, as defined by Aristotle, is "an imitation of a noble and complete action" that "achieves, through the representation of pitiable and fearful incidents, the catharsis of such incidents" (*Poetics*, chap. 6). How does *Macbeth* function as a tragedy?

Answer Key for *Macbeth*

Note to Teachers: This answer key can be removed before the study guide is given to the student.

STUDY QUESTIONS

Part One—Knowledge of the Text

1. Thane of Cawdor

2. They greet Macbeth as "Thane of Glamis" (his current title), "Thane of Cawdor", and "King hereafter", and they prophesy that Banquo will be the father of kings.

3. Macbeth

4. Macduff

5. Lady Macbeth's

6. Donalbain's

7. His grooms/attendants

8. The three witches

9. The first apparition, an armed head, warns Macbeth to "Beware Macduff; / Beware the Thane of Fife"; Macbeth is killed by Macduff in the final act. The second apparition, a bloody child, declares that "none of woman born / Shall harm Macbeth"; Macduff reveals that he was "untimely ripp'd" from his mother's womb. The third apparition, a child crowned with a tree in his hand, pronounces that Macbeth will not be vanquished until "[g]reat Birnam wood to high Dunsinane Hill / Shall come against him"; all of Malcolm's men cut down branches from Birnam Wood and carry them before them into battle to conceal the true size of their army.

10. Ross

11. Seyton

12. Lady Macbeth's

13. It is rumored to be suicide, though her death occurs offstage.

14. Macbeth's

15. Macduff

Part Two—Essay Questions

1. *What is the nature of courage? What is the nature of ambition? How are both used throughout the play for different ends?*

   This essay should address the more obvious examples of Macbeth and of Lady Macbeth but could also fruitfully reflect on other characters: Macduff, Lady Macduff, and their son; Banquo and Fleance; Duncan and his sons; etc. Clear definitions of courage and ambition should serve as the foundation for a careful examination of all of the characters and actions within the play. The presence or lack of these qualities should be considered. Is initiative the same thing as courage? Are fortitude and courage the same thing? Are boldness and courage the same thing? Is resolve a conduit for or a barrier to courage? Who is ambitious in the play, and what are the results of ambitious actions?

2. *What does Macbeth's military prowess signify for his character? Does the image of him as "Bellona's bridegroom" (1.2.55) develop across the play?*

   The simplest (but not necessarily the most accurate or illuminating) path for this essay is simply to see Macbeth's military prowess as a harbinger of his bloody-minded capacity later in the play. Beyond this, however, the essay should examine heroism and nobility carefully and see how such attributes can or cannot be seen in Macbeth. The difference between reported

virtue and actual virtue should be noted. Is a degree of nobility at the start of a play necessary for the descent of a soul
toward death and despair to be effectively tragic? If so, how
does Macbeth's readiness to entertain the option of murder
reflect on his "degree" of nobility? Another pathway that could
be followed here as well would be to consider Macbeth's other
"bride" and her effect on his character (heroic or otherwise).

3. *What is the nature of the relationship between Macbeth and
   Lady Macbeth? Directors have frequently presented them in early
   scenes as an affectionate couple; is this reading an appropriate
   one? How—if at all—does their relationship change over the
   course of the play?*

   The writer of this essay should have a working familiar-
   ity with varying answers commonly made to this question
   (particularly with regard to an overly romanticized vision of
   the marriage) but should at the same time work to answer the
   question through close adherence to the play itself. An undue
   emphasis on "gender" issues may weaken an argument unless
   it is supported by a carefully researched understanding of the
   text. The language used by both characters toward each other
   while together and regarding each other while apart should
   be contrasted. Is Lady Macbeth a greater or a lesser influence
   on her husband than are the three witches? Why will he not
   discuss the plot to kill Banquo with her? Why does she run
   mad and commit suicide—and why is Macbeth seemingly
   not aware of her rapid decline?

4. *Consider how rapidly Macbeth and his wife both leap to the
   option of murder when considering their path to the throne.
   What does this rapidity in forming the intention and means for
   murder demonstrate about their characters?*

   Understanding of the process entailed in a moral action would
   serve this essay well. Its primary consideration should be a
   methodical analysis of moments in the plot where Macbeth

and Lady Macbeth ponder situations and first announce their solutions (e.g., for realizing the witches' prophecy by removing Duncan). Examination of other characters (especially Macduff, Banquo, and Malcolm) as a counterpoint to this discussion would also be appropriate. Particular questions may also be considered. Why is Lady Macbeth plagued with guilt-ridden sleepwalking, while her husband (whose apparent squeamishness earlier in the play earned his wife's vocal scorn) brazenly continues in his tyrannical killing spree? Is her emphasis on resolve and boldness demonstrative of strength or weakness?

5. *What is the function of the occult in* Macbeth*? How is it presented? What is its effect on characters, and in terms of staging, what would its effect possibly be on the audience? How does the presence of the witches work in the context of a possible moral message in the play?*

This essay should discuss the high-fantastical setting of *Macbeth* in great detail, as well as the characters of the witches. It would be interesting, but not at all necessary, to investigate King James' *Daemonologie.* Does the theatricality of the evil make it more vivid or more distant? How is the dreamlike and unclear effect of the supernatural on the human scene analogous to the vision of the world through the eyes of a man with disordered passions? In practical terms, how could or should the play be staged? Cinematically inclined students can refer to Bemis' essay or their own knowledge of adaptations of the play.

6. *Consider the characters of men—such as Banquo and Lennox— who are not at the forefront either of Macbeth's usurpation or of Malcolm's reclamation of the throne. What degrees of moral culpability are there between resistance or defiance and submission or compromise?*

In the consideration of these characters, their motivations and actions need to be taken into account. How do they behave toward the three kings placed over them—Duncan, Macbeth, and (as the play's conclusion implies) Malcolm? What is their sense of loyalty? What is their sense of ambition? How long does it take them to recognize dangers or weaknesses in a monarch? With regard to Banquo in particular, his place in Shakespeare's source (Holingshed's *Chronicles*) as an accomplice to the murder of Duncan might be mentioned. Lee Oser's essay, "The Vision of Evil in *Macbeth*", could also be reviewed.

7. *What is the purpose of the unseen presence of King Edward the Confessor? What does his character demonstrate in terms of an ideal vision of the monarchy? For whom is he a fitting counterpoint?*

    This essay should first provide a clear account of King Edward the Confessor as portrayed in the play—his miraculous healing of subjects afflicted with "the king's evil" (scrofula) by his royal touch—as well as explore larger questions of governance, monarchical responsibilities and powers, and belief in the divine right of kings. The obvious contrast between the bloody hands of Macbeth and the healing hands of King Edward should be noted and explored more fully. The image Malcolm draws of himself as an evil, vice-ridden king is also pertinent, especially because of his demonstrable virtues. The larger historical context may also be considered with regard to the reigns of both Elizabeth and James I.

8. *The play concludes with the routing of the tyrant Macbeth and the crowning of Malcolm as king. How does the character of Malcolm measure up to notions of kingship represented throughout the play? Will he be a good king?*

    In a similar way to the essay on King Edward the Confessor, this essay should explore questions concerning the monarchy. Analysis of Duncan as king may prove useful as well. When is a king strong, and when is he weak? Is it weakness to be blind to the deceitful machinations of those you love and trust? Particular attention should be paid to Malcolm's conversation with Macduff in Act 4, scene 3, regarding the virtues—or vices—of a king. It would be interesting as well to discuss the difference between the military heroism attributed to Macbeth, and Malcolm's management of his forces at the end of the play.

9. *What is the role of blood in the play, especially in reference to the deaths that occur offstage?*

   Blood is specifically mentioned a startling number of times in the play, from the bloody sergeant who comes to tell Duncan of the victories over Macdonwald and the king of Norway (1.2.1) to the sanguinely soaked final acts of scene 5. It represents life, death, murder, kinships, suffering, and guilt. Any or all of these elements can be explored in this essay. Which deaths occur onstage, and which occur offstage? As their hands are stained with blood, are the sins of Macbeth and Lady Macbeth irredeemable?

10. *Tragedy, as defined by Aristotle, is "an imitation of a noble and complete action" that "achieves, through the representation of pitiable and fearful incidents, the catharsis of such incidents" (Poetics, chap. 6). How does* Macbeth *function as a tragedy?*

    Addressing this question will require a careful consideration of the play as a whole, especially in terms of the moral message(s) it articulates with regard to sin and the perversion of the human soul. The question of fate and its role with regard to free will should also be addressed. The nobility of Macbeth—or, more specifically, the fact that he *could* have been redeemed—is an important component in qualifying the play as a tragedy. Pearce's description of the play as a "tragedy of errors" could also provide important food for thought here; likewise, a more detailed reading of Aristotle's *Poetics*, chapter 6, could prove fruitful.

Notes

———————*Notes*———————